FOOTBALL L

MARY FOWLER

First published by Albert Street Books, an imprint of Allen & Unwin, in 2024

Copyright © Text, Allen & Unwin 2024
Copyright © Illustrations, Leigh Hedstrom 2024

All rights reserved. No part of this book may be reproduced or transmitted in any form or by any means, electronic or mechanical, including photocopying, recording or by any information storage and retrieval system, without prior permission in writing from the publisher. The Australian *Copyright Act 1968* (the Act) allows a maximum of one chapter or ten per cent of this book, whichever is the greater, to be photocopied by any educational institution for its educational purposes provided that the educational institution (or body that administers it) has given a remuneration notice to the Copyright Agency (Australia) under the Act.

Allen & Unwin
Cammeraygal Country
83 Alexander Street
Crows Nest NSW 2065
Australia
Phone: (61 2) 8425 0100
Email: info@allenandunwin.com
Web: www.allenandunwin.com

Allen & Unwin acknowledges the Traditional Owners of the Country on which we live and work. We pay our respects to all Aboriginal and Torres Strait Islander Elders, past and present.

 A catalogue record for this book is available from the National Library of Australia

ISBN 978 1 76118 134 4

For teaching resources, explore allenandunwin.com/learn

Cover design by Hana Kinoshita Thomson
Cover photo by Speed Media / Alamy Stock Photo
Text design by Hana Kinoshita Thomson
Set in 14 pt Urbane Rounded Medium
Printed and bound in Australia by the Opus Group

This is an independent and unofficial work. Any names, characters, trademarks, service marks and trade names referred to in this book are the property of their respective owners and are used solely for identification and reference purposes. This book is a publication of Allen & Unwin Pty Ltd and has not been licensed, approved, sponsored or endorsed by any person or entity.

10 9 8 7 6 5 4 3 2 1

CONTENTS

CHAPTER 1: There's Something About Mary........1

CHAPTER 2: The Fowler Five........................13

CHAPTER 3: Trials and Travels....................23

CHAPTER 4: Soccer Smarts........................37

CHAPTER 5: Going Pro.............................49

CHAPTER 6: Man City..............................59

CHAPTER 7: Playing for Australia................71

CHAPTER 8: Dream Come True.....................83

CHAPTER 9: Fowler Fever.........................95

CHAPTER 10: The Legendary Mary Fowler........109

CHAPTER ONE

THERE'S SOMETHING ABOUT MARY

Hi there. I'm Gary the G.O.A.T.

Ha-ha – no, I'm not the **Greatest. Of. All. Time,** although my mum says I am.

She also calls me **G-GOAT (Gary – Gorgeous Outstanding And Talented).**

But you know who *is* a

REAL LIFE LEGEND?

Football player MARY FOWLER

And this book is all about her!

Mary has got incredible

TECHNICAL SKILLS

on the soccer field!

She is **FAST** and **ATHLETIC** and works hard to keep fit.

She is **CLEVER** and **STRATEGIC,** calculating the best moves for the **WHOLE TEAM.**

She is **MENTALLY TOUGH** and keeps it together even in the most high-pressure competitions like the **World Cup** or the **Olympics.**

'She is so good out there, on and off the ball, the way she sets players up, her movement — she's floating...'

TONY GUSTAVSSON,
head coach of the Matildas

WHAT MAKES MARY SUCH A LEGEND ON THE FIELD?

DRIBBLING

Outstanding at close ball control, Mary dribbles past her opponents creating **goal opportunities** and **breaking through defensive lines.**

FINISHING

Whether it's a **precise shot,** or a **header,** or some other creative finish, Mary is a big threat when **she gets a chance to score.**

SPEED

Fast and agile, Mary constantly **outsmarts her opponents** in defence.

GAME AWARENESS

She **closely watches the field** and **plans ahead** to set up scoring opportunities for the team.

MENTAL STRENGTH

Tough and resilient, Mary stays **calm and focused** when the pressure is on.

Name: Mary Boio Fowler

Date of Birth: 14 February 2003 (Valentine's Day!)

Place of Birth: Cairns, QLD (Gimuy, Yidinji country)

Height: 1.72m

Position: Striker

Preferred Foot: Both!

Number: 11 for Australia, 8 for Manchester City WFC

Position: Striker and mid-fielder

Nicknames: Maz / Star Girl

Clubs: Manchester City WFC, Montpellier HSC, Bankstown City FC, Illawarra Stingrays, Adelaide United

National team: Matildas

Mary's **versatility** makes her a very valuable player.

She can play **multiple positions** in the **attacking third,** such as a **striker, winger,** or **attacking midfielder,** and adjusts quickly to different tactical setups.

She can even **play with both feet!**

'She's like one of the most **AMAZING** players in our team. She's **20 years old** and has a head on her like she's 30 and **been around the game for 100 years.**'

SAM KERR, captain of the Matildas

CHAPTER TWO

THE FOWLER FIVE

Mary Fowler was born in **Cairns/Gimuy** in Far North Queensland.

Cairns is a **warm, tropical city** close to the famous **Great Barrier Reef**, one of the **seven natural wonders** of the world.

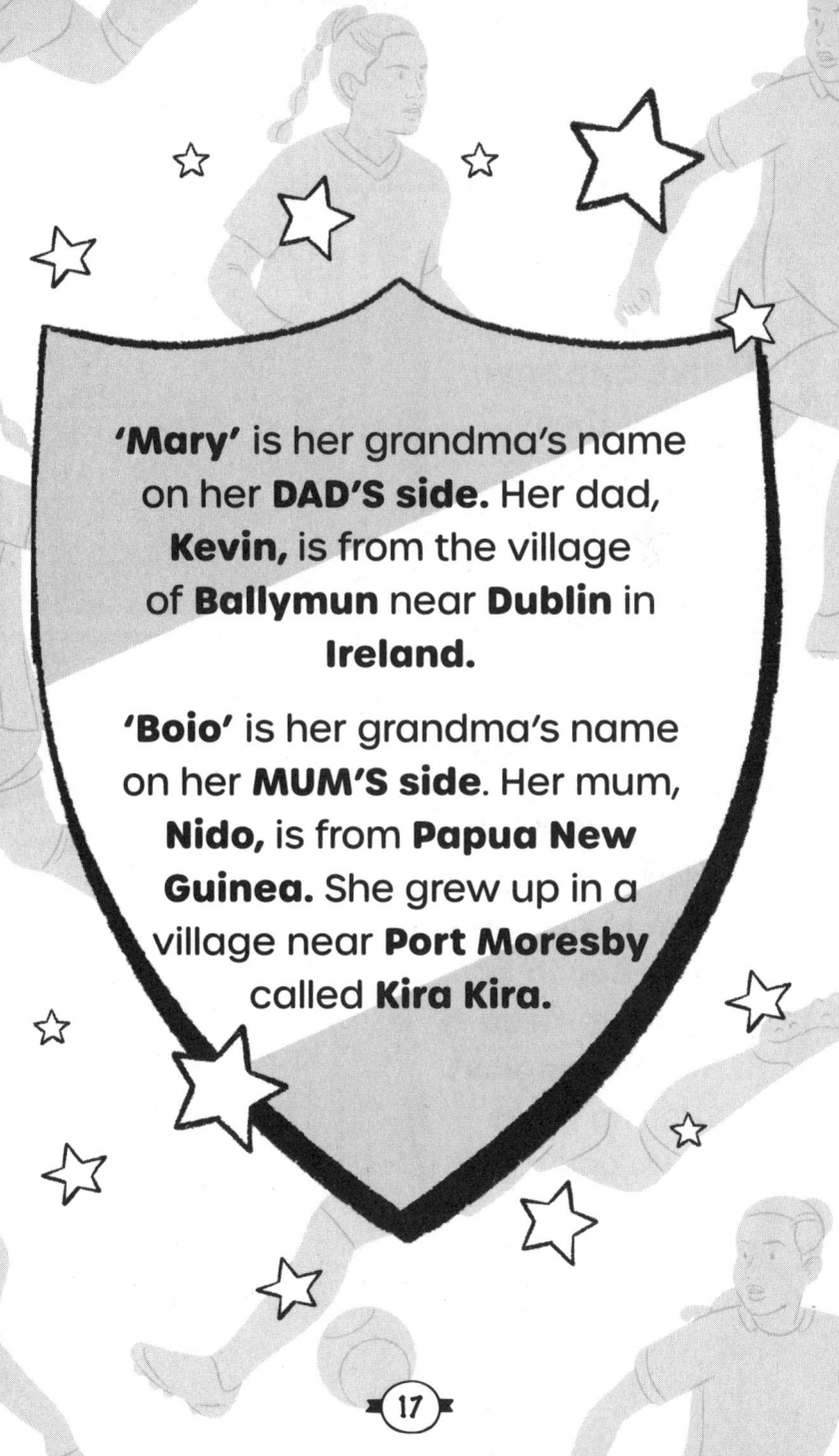

'**Mary**' is her grandma's name on her **DAD'S side.** Her dad, **Kevin,** is from the village of **Ballymun** near **Dublin** in **Ireland.**

'**Boio**' is her grandma's name on her **MUM'S side**. Her mum, **Nido,** is from **Papua New Guinea.** She grew up in a village near **Port Moresby** called **Kira Kira.**

Fowler Five

Mary is the **middle** of **FIVE CHILDREN**. All of them **LOVE soccer!**

FUN TIMES

Mary's parents decided not to have a TV at home, but the **Fowler Five** found plenty of ways to have fun.

MINI-OLYMPICS

After school the whole family would drive to nearby **Trinity Beach** and go head-to-head in a **'mini-Olympics'**, running races and kicking a ball around.

HOMEWORK

Sometimes they would have their **dinner on the beach** and the kids would do their **homework** right there **on the sand.**

Mary is **REALLY PROUD** of her **mixed heritage.** When she was fifteen, she faced a **BIG decision.**

Her **older brother Caoimhìn** and **sister Ciara** have both played for **Ireland's youth international teams.** The Irish World Cup women's team (also known as the **Girls in Green**) desperately wanted Mary to join their squad and **represent Ireland** as well.

Mary was torn.

'We all want to play together for the same country. Family is really important to me, it's important to all of us.'

MARY FOWLER

In the end she decided to go with **THE MATILDAS.**

'I do feel very **connected to both my parents' backgrounds,** and I don't see myself as just an Australian. I see myself as Papuan and Irish too.'

MARY FOWLER

PHEEEE-EW!

CHAPTER THREE

TRIALS AND TRAVELS

Mary started playing soccer when she was **seven.**

She was a member of the **boys' team** for **SAINTS FC,** and also played for **LEICHHARDT FC** in the local **Cairns league.**

At **ten years old,** Mary was selected to play for the **QUEENSLAND U-12** team. She was playing against **boys two years older** than her!

Mary also likes **drawing** and **writing poetry,** and she used to **dress up** and **act out little shows** for her parents.

⚽ Just before she started high school, the family moved to the **Netherlands** for **three years** and Mary played for the **BVV BARENDRECHT team.**

⚽ While she was there she learned to speak the **Dutch language!**

LEGENDE!!!
(that's LEGEND in **Dutch**)

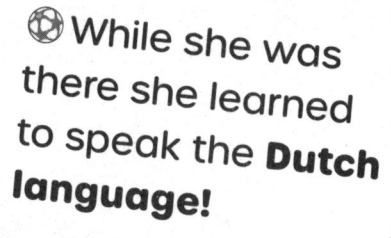

People often say that Brazilian **MARTA VIEIRA DA SILVA** is the greatest female footballer of all time.

Mary loves Marta's **bold creativity** and she models her **playing style** on her.

'We're both **DRIBBLERS**,' says MARY.

That sounds messy!

The **Fowlers** moved back to **Australia** when **Mary was 14.**

She played for the

ILLAWARRA STINGRAYS

and then

BANKSTOWN CITY FC

in the

NSW WOMEN'S NATIONAL PREMIER LEAGUE

In 2019, when Mary was **only 16,** she signed a **contract** with

ADELAIDE UNITED FC

and **moved AGAIN** – this time to **South Australia.**

35

Mary was now playing in the country's **premier women's soccer competition**, the

A-LEAGUE WOMEN.

This was the official start of her

PROFESSIONAL FOOTBALL CAREER!

CHAPTER FOUR

SOCCER SMARTS

Soccer is the **MOST POPULAR SPORT** in the world! More than **250 million people** in over **200 countries and territories** play the game.

Modern soccer is said to have been born in **England** in **1863,** but the earliest versions of the game can be traced back to **over 2000 years ago** in **Ancient China.**

The **aim of the game** is to **score goals** by **kicking the ball** into the opposing team's **goal.** The team with the **most goals** at the end of the game **wins.**

An **international** soccer game is **90 minutes long.** The 90 minutes is divided in **two 45-minute halves.**

PITCH or FIELD

In **England** and **Europe** the ground where soccer is played is called the **PITCH.**

In **America** and **Australia** and **Canada** it's called the **PLAYING FIELD.**

Confusion!

FOOTBALL or SOCCER

Most of the world calls the sport **FOOTBALL**, but in **Australia** and **Canada** and the **USA**, it's called **SOCCER**.

MORE confusion!

FOUL FACTS

The following actions are **not allowed** in soccer:

- **Kicking** an opponent
- **Tripping**
- **Jumping** or **charging** into an opponent
- **Pushing**
- **Tackling from behind**
- **Holding**
- **Touching** the ball **with your hands** (if you are not the goalkeeper)

If a player does any of these during a game, the **referee** can deliver a **penalty.** Penalties can range from the opposing team getting a **free kick** to the fouling player getting a **caution** or **expulsion** from the game.

Yellow card: the card shown to a player on their first caution, warning them not to do that action again.

Careful: two yellow cards in a match = **a red card!**

Red card: the card shown to a player on their second caution. The player is disqualified and must leave the field.

There are **NO SUBSTITUTES** for players who get red cards, so the **whole team suffers** because they have **ONE LESS** player than the other team.

The **maximum number** of **players** on a soccer team is **11**.

The different positions are:

- Goalkeeper
- Centre-back
- Sweeper
- Fullback
- Wingback
- Central midfielder
- Defensive midfielder
- Attacking midfielder
- Winger
- Forward
- Striker

In a professional match there is **one head referee** and at least **two assistant referees.** They enforce the rules and make sure play is fair.

> Remember, the referee always has the final say. If you argue with the referee, you could get a yellow or red card!

TIME FOR A FIELD TRIP

Soccer field:
90 – 120m long by 45 – 90m wide

Rugby field:
approx. 100m long by 68m wide

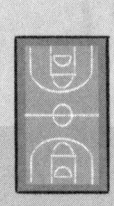

Basketball court:
28m long by
15m wide

**Aussie Rules
Football oval:**
135 – 185m long by
110 – 155m wide

★ BALL BASICS ★

All **regulation soccer balls** must be:

- ⚽ **spherical**

- ⚽ made of **suitable materials** such as **latex, rubber** and **leather** (in Europe, during the Middle Ages, soccer balls were made from **inflated pig bladders!**)

- ⚽ of a **circumference** between **68cm** and **70cm**

- ⚽ between **410g** and **450g** in **weight** at the start of the match

- ⚽ of a **pressure** equal to **0.6-1.1 bars** at sea level

- ⚽ **officially tested**

CHAPTER FIVE

GOING PRO

LEGENDARY GAME

MARY'S FIRST ★ PRO GAME ★

Who? Adelaide United FC vs Western Sydney Wanderers

Where? Marconi Stadium, Sydney

Why was it legendary? Mary made her A-League Women debut in the first game of the **2019-2020** season. A big bonus was her **sister Ciara,** who plays midfield, also signed with the Adelaide club.

They made their club debuts in the same game on the same side! They lost the game, but **Mary scored her first goal.**

One month before Mary turned 17, she signed a **three-year contract** with a team in the **French Ligue 1 club** called **Montpellier Hérault Sport Club.**

'This is a **great opportunity** for Mary and something that can **propel her career** even further.'

IVAN KARLOVIĆ, head of Women's Football at Adelaide United

Mary moved all the way to France alone.

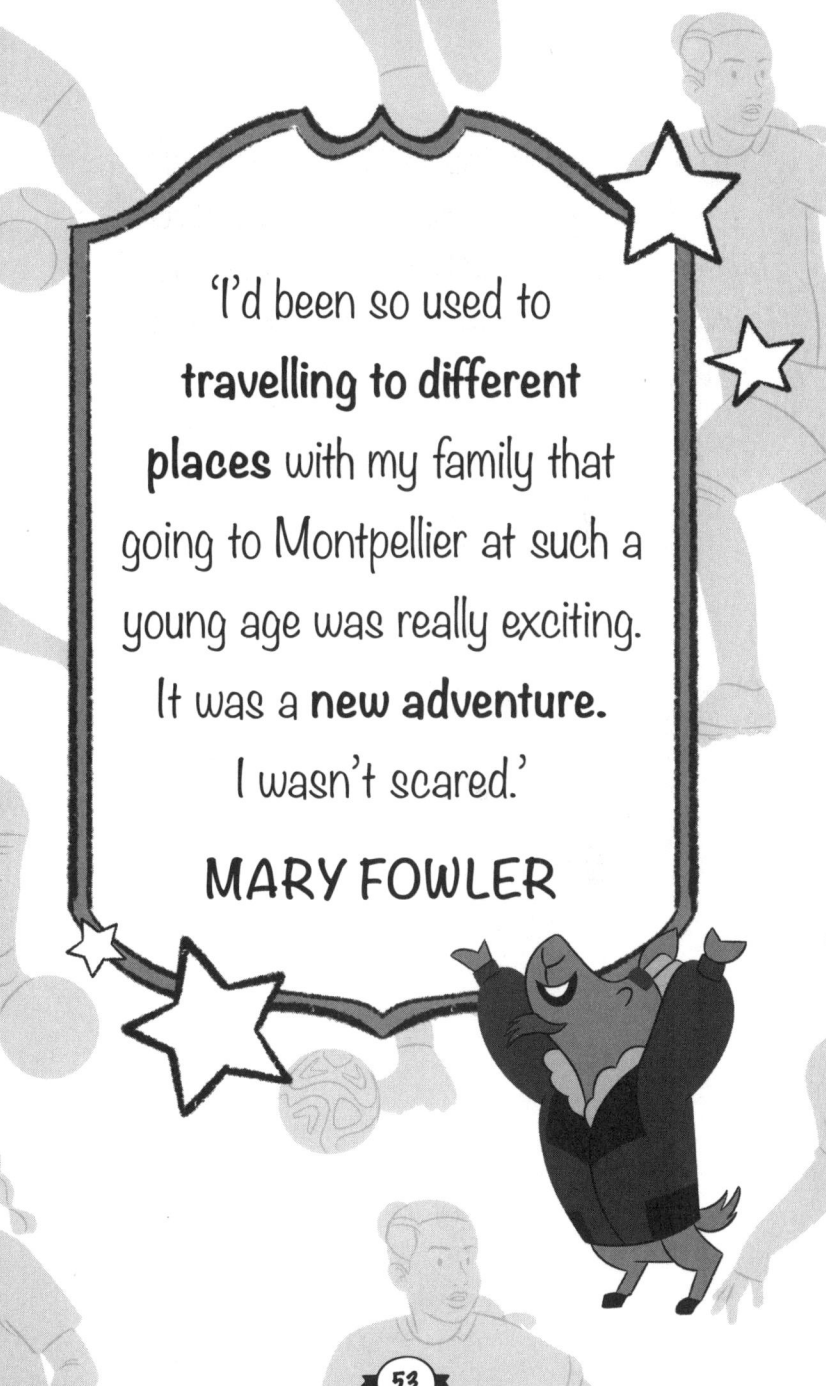

'I'd been so used to **travelling to different places** with my family that going to Montpellier at such a young age was really exciting. It was a **new adventure.** I wasn't scared.'

MARY FOWLER

At **Montpellier HSC,** Mary played against some of the **best footballers in the world** and continued to **develop her skills.**

In the **2020-21 season,** she was in the **starting squad** for multiple games, and was really good at **putting the ball in the back of the net.**

It seemed like things were going well, but **Mary's first season in Europe** was affected by **Covid-19!**

She **couldn't play** as much, and she **couldn't travel,** so she **didn't see her family** in Australia for **THREE YEARS.**

It was tough.

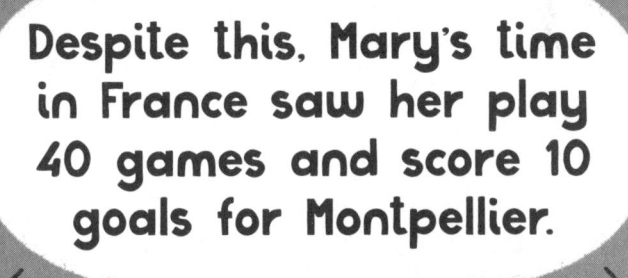

Despite this, Mary's time in France saw her play 40 games and score 10 goals for Montpellier.

'It's been **a long time** since you've seen a player possess such **natural striker instincts.** It's something that's very difficult to teach, and she's got that – **at a young age.'**

IVAN KARLOVIĆ,
head of Women's Football at Adelaide United

CHAPTER SIX

MAN CITY

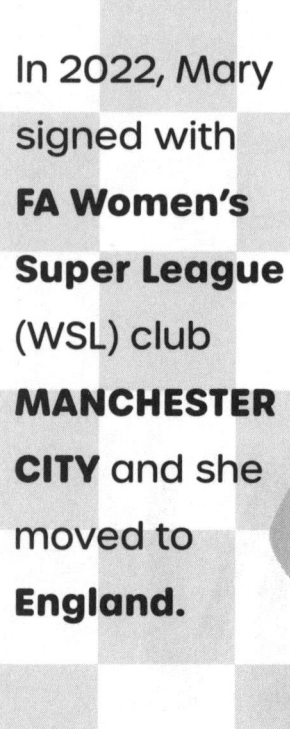

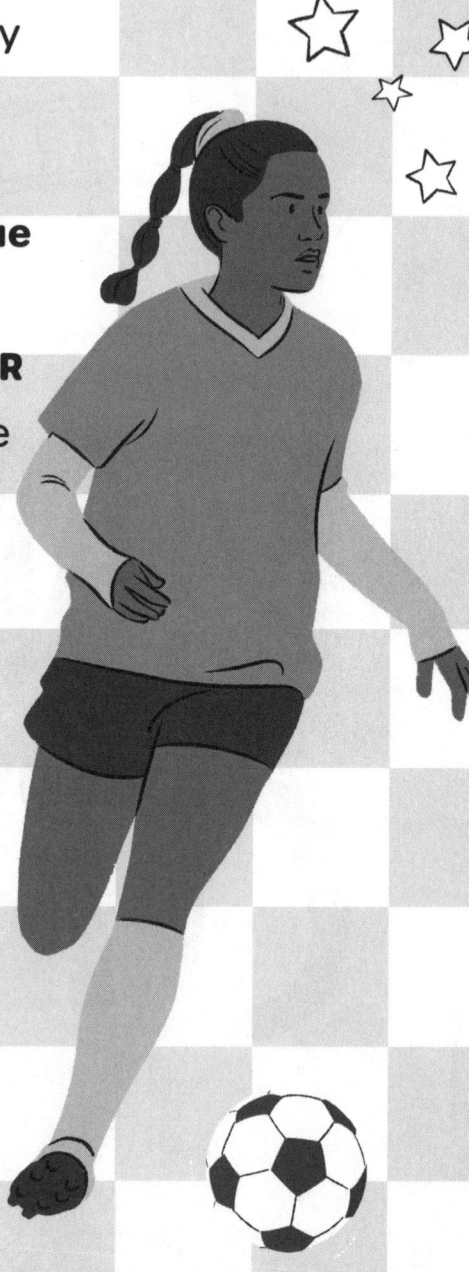

In 2022, Mary signed with **FA Women's Super League** (WSL) club **MANCHESTER CITY** and she moved to **England.**

'I'm still young and **I've got a lot to learn,** so being at a club like **City** where I'll be surrounded by **amazing staff and coaches,** as well as playing alongside and against some of the best players in the world, I feel that **I have everything I need to fulfil my potential.'**

MARY FOWLER

She scored her **FIRST goal** for the club, **a penalty,** in a game against the **Blackburn Rovers.**

Then she scored her **SECOND goal** 29 minutes later!

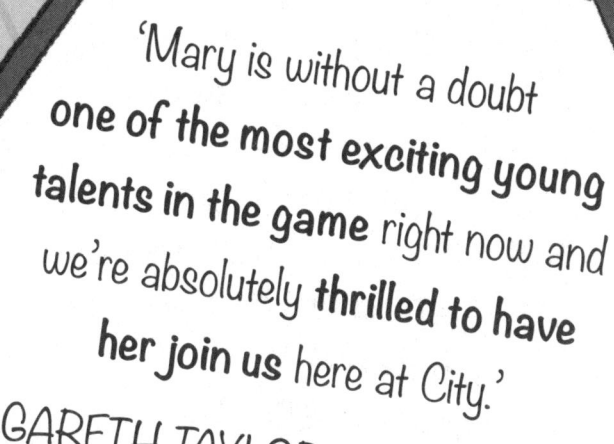

'Mary is without a doubt **one of the most exciting young talents in the game** right now and we're absolutely **thrilled to have her join us** here at City.'

GARETH TAYLOR, head coach of Manchester City Women

In her **first season,** Mary was given **165 minutes of play** across **11 WSL games** with **no starts.** She was a new player to the club and had to prove herself. The following season, however, she played **225 minutes** in her **first three games** and **started** the match!

So far, Mary has made **52 appearances** for **Manchester City** and has scored **11 goals.**

Not a bad start!

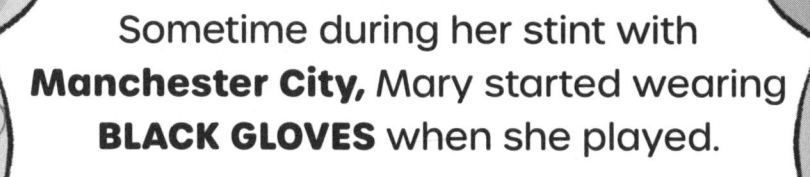

Sometime during her stint with **Manchester City,** Mary started wearing **BLACK GLOVES** when she played.

It was a **BIG MYSTERY** and social media was **buzzing** about it.

⚽ Is she practising to be a goalkeeper one day?

⚽ Is she trying to start a new fashion for soccer players?

⚽ Is it too cold in England for her?

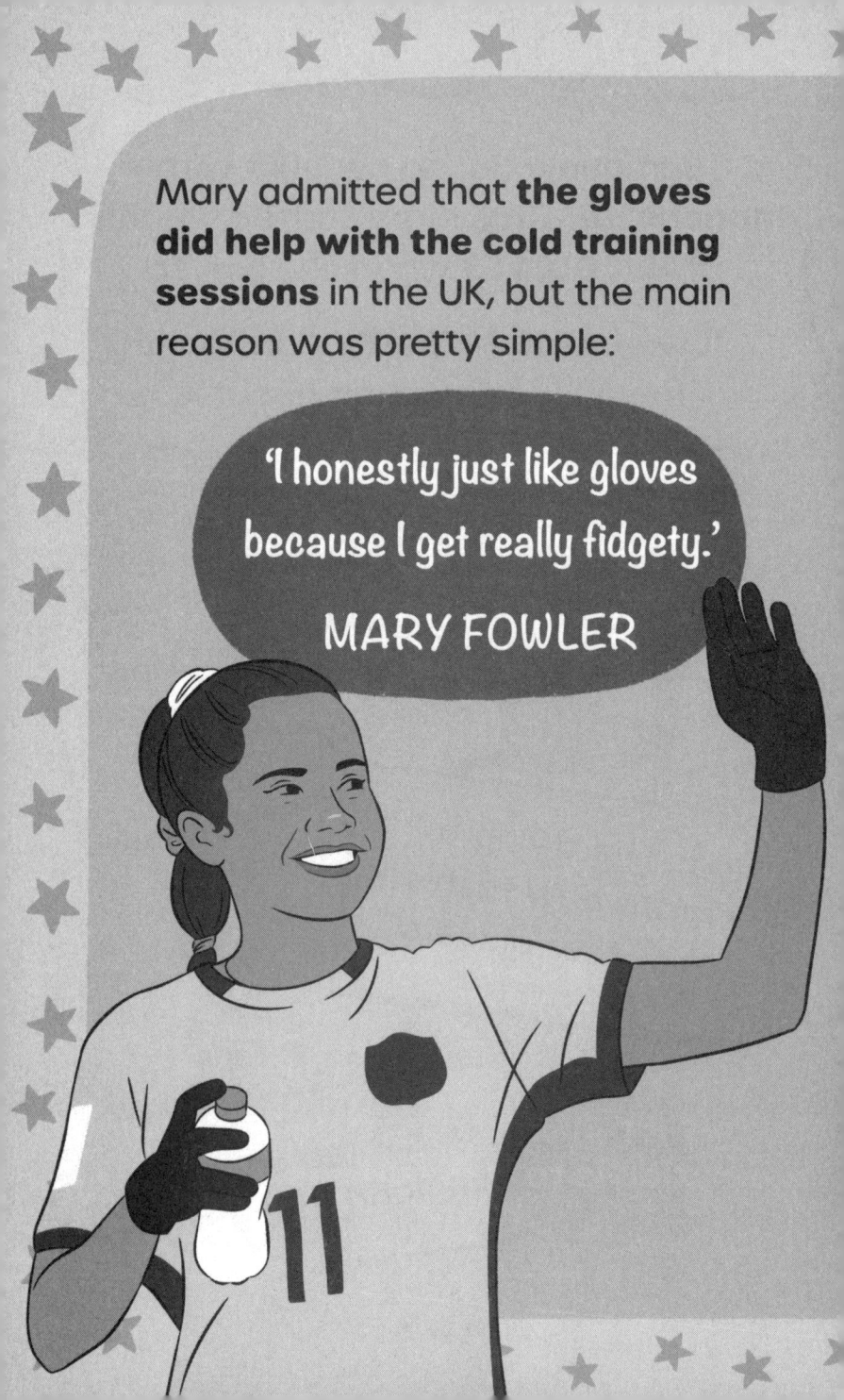

Mary admitted that **the gloves did help with the cold training sessions** in the UK, but the main reason was pretty simple:

'I honestly just like gloves because I get really fidgety.'

MARY FOWLER

Hmmm, gloves would look awesome with my jacket…

When Mary is training, **she fiddles with a ring on her finger** to help get out her **nervous energy.** However, players are not allowed to wear jewellery during a game. **Her solution is to wear gloves.**

One of the **best things** about moving to **Manchester** was that Mary could see her **grandpa** more often. **Ireland** was much closer now – only **266 kilometres** away!

After one game between **Australia** and **Ireland** (where **she scored twice!**), Mary went over to **Grandpa Fowler** who was watching in the stands.

She gave him her **Matildas jersey** and a **GREAT BIG HUG.** Everybody cheered!
FOWLER
11

Mary is all about **positive vibes!**
She has two quotes she likes to live by:

'Be the energy you want to attract.'

'Everything is figureoutable.'

'Just believing that if I gave **good energy** then good things would come back to me.'

MARY FOWLER

CHAPTER SEVEN

PLAYING FOR AUSTRALIA

As Mary's club career **gained momentum,** so too did her **international career!**

Let's wind back the clock a bit!

⚽ Mary began training with the **Young Matildas** when she was **14**.

She played her **first game** for the **Matildas** in **2018** at the **TOURNAMENT OF NATIONS**.

Mary **ran on in stoppage** time for the **final minutes** of the game against **Brazil,** so she didn't play for long, but she was still part of their **LEGENDARY 3-1 win.**

Mary's international debut made her the **fifth youngest player** for the Matildas!

'[She has] probably got the **most weapons** I've seen from a **young player** her age in **women's football.**'

ALEN STAJCIC, head coach of the Matildas 2014-2019

Matilda's Youngest Players

1. 14 years 240 days: **Sharon Wass** (1981)

2. 14 years 343 days: **Kelly Golebiowski** (1996)

3. 15 years 133 days: **Jenna Kingsley** (2007)

4. 15 years 150 days: **Sam Kerr** (2009)

5. 15 years 162 days: **Mary Fowler** (2018)

Mary was called up for the **2019 FIFA WORLD CUP** when she was just 16 – the youngest member on the squad.

But before she could play, **she injured her hamstring.** By the time she was better the **Matildas had been knocked out of the competition,** so she never got to make her tournament debut.

BUMMER!

Still, **it was an important learning experience for her.** She got to be right in the middle of a major competition without the pressure of playing, and **she got to train with the most AWESOME Aussie team ever!**

The **2019 FIFA World Cup** was held in **France.**

24 teams played **52 matches** across **9 cities.**

Over 1 billion people tuned in to watch from all **around the world!**

Qualified Teams

Australia	Brazil
China	Chile
Japan	New Zealand
South Korea	England
Thailand	France
Cameroon	Germany
Nigeria	Italy
South Africa	Netherlands
Canada	Norway
Jamaica	Scotland
United States	Spain
Argentina	Sweden

FIFA FACTS

FIFA stands for the **'Fédération Internationale de Football Association'**.

The first official **Women's World Cup tournament** was held in **1991 in China,** and was won by the **United States.**

Twelve teams entered in **1991**. By **2023**, the field had expanded to **32 teams.**

Marta Vieira da Silva holds the record for the **most goals scored** in Women's World Cup history, with **17 goals.**

So far, **five countries** have won the Women's World Cup – the **United States, Germany, Norway, Japan** and **Spain.**

Since **1995,** Australia has **qualified** for **every FIFA Women's World Cup** (1995, 1999, 2003, 2007, 2011, 2015, 2019 and 2023).

The **1995** FIFA Women's World Cup was also the **first tournament** at which the team was called **the 'Matildas'.** Before that, they were referred to as the **'Female Socceroos'.**

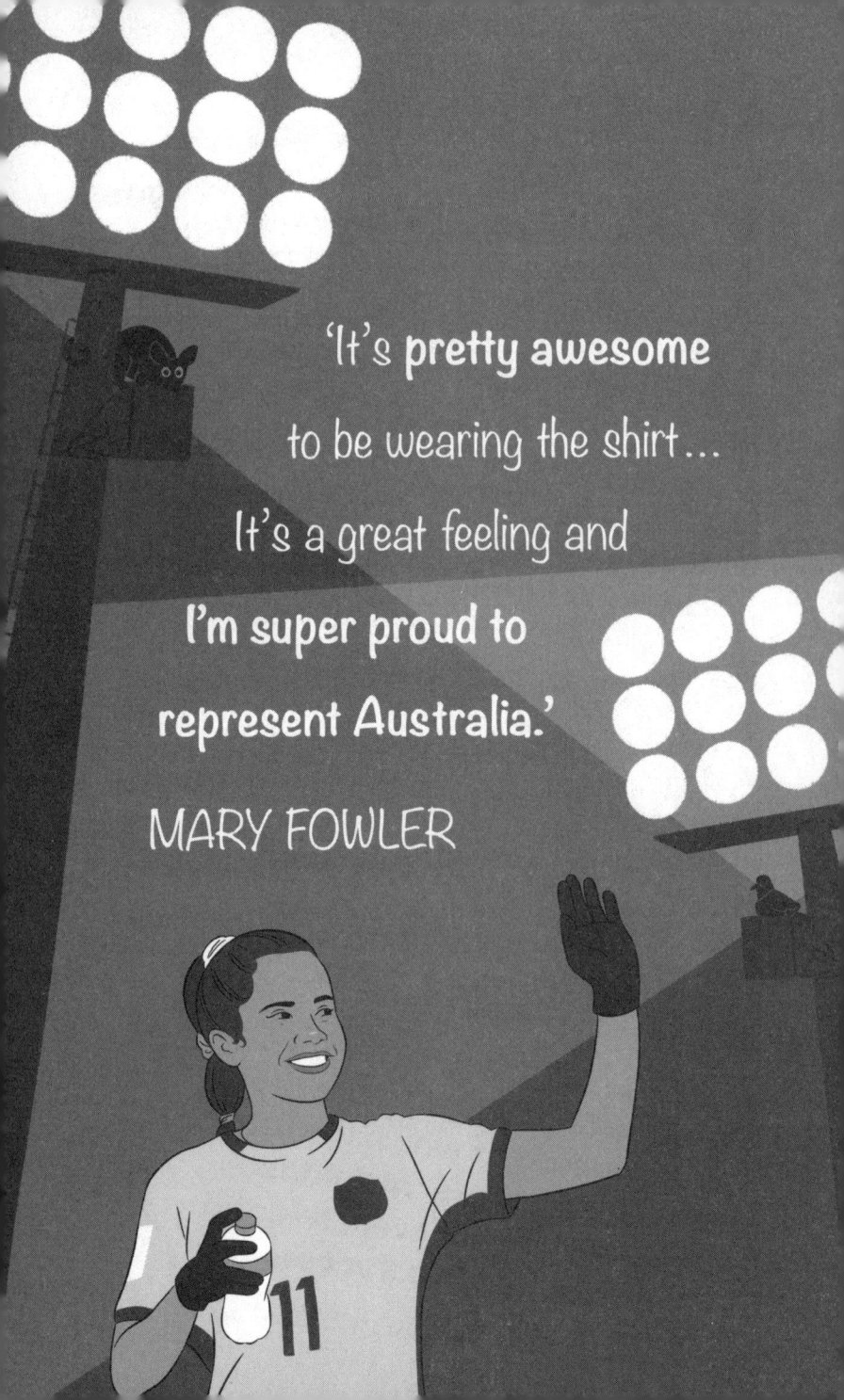

'It's **pretty awesome** to be wearing the shirt… It's a great feeling and **I'm super proud to** represent Australia.'

MARY FOWLER

CHAPTER EIGHT

DREAM COME TRUE

When Mary was a little girl playing soccer on **Trinity Beach** with her family, her one **big dream** was to compete in the **Olympic Games.**

Her dream came true in 2020, when Mary was selected to play for **the Matildas** at the **2020 Tokyo Olympics!**

> 'It feels absolutely amazing to be selected for the **Tokyo 2020 Olympics.** As a kid, it was the one dream I had in sports, so it feels amazing.'
>
> MARY FOWLER

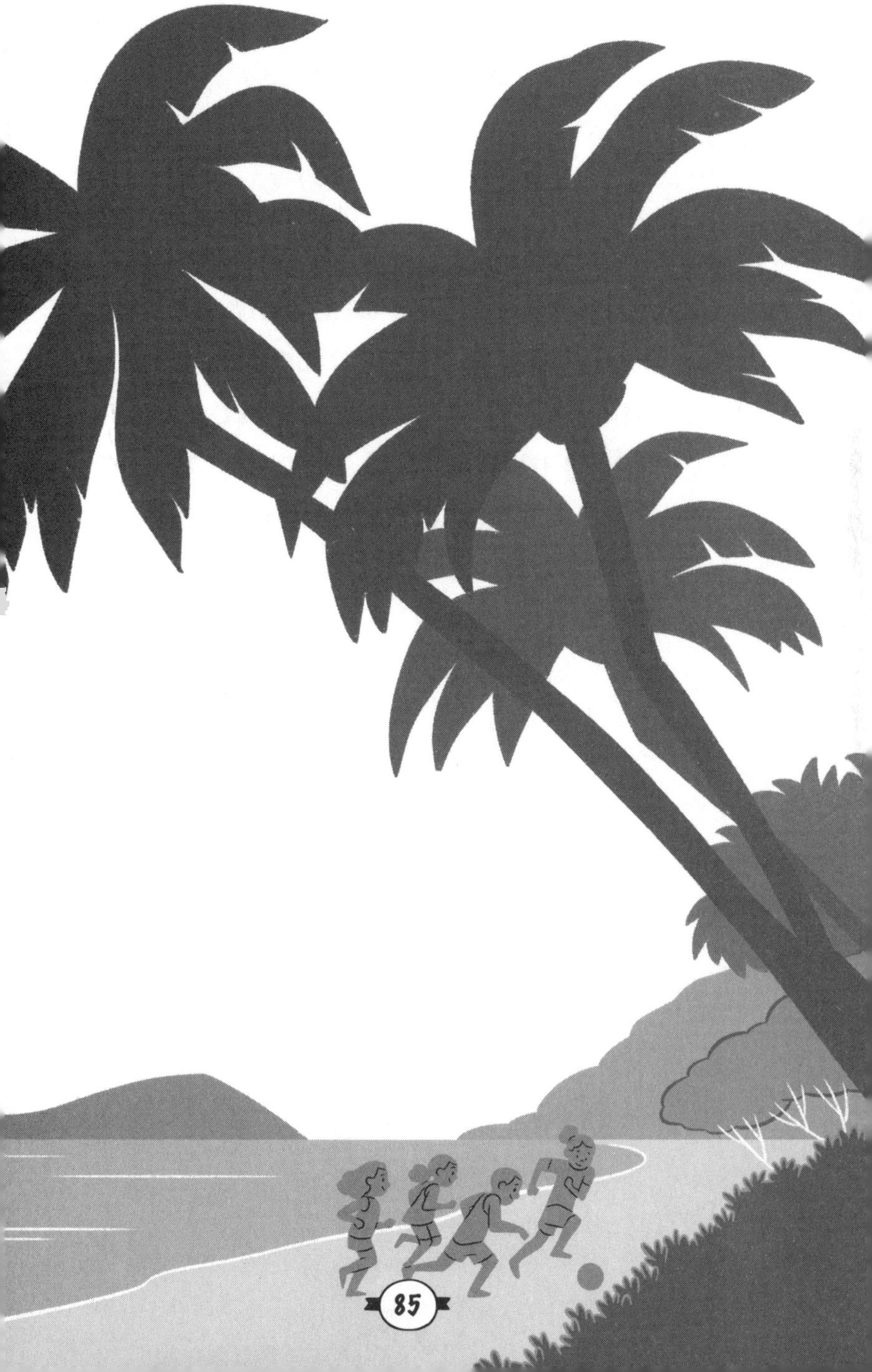

Mary made her **Olympic debut** in a **Group G match** against **New Zealand.** The Matildas **won their opening match 2-1,** scoring twice in the first half and **keeping their lead for the rest of the game.**

⚽ **Group G** had some **heavyweights,** and the Matildas were in for a challenge!

New Zealand

Sweden

United States of America

LEGENDARY GAME: OLYMPIC GOOOOAL

⚽ WHO?
Matildas vs Great Britain

⚽ WHERE?
Kashima Soccer Stadium, Japan

⚽ WHY WAS IT LEGENDARY?

The Matildas made it to the **quarter-finals** and faced **Great Britain.** The match went into extra time, and **Mary scored a goal in the 104th minute** with a **left-foot missile** that bounced off a defender and landed in the back of the net. **Australia won 4-3.**

> 'I didn't even know what happened, it just went in!'
>
> MARY FOWLER

When she looks back on that day, she still gets **goosebumps.**

レジェンド
(that's LEGEND in Japanese)

The Matildas narrowly missed out on the bronze medal in a **close match against USA** where they **lost 4-3.**

But their **fourth-place finish** was their most **successful performance** at any **Olympic Games** so far.

THE MATILDAS MADE ALL OF AUSTRALIA PROUD WITH THEIR HISTORIC ACHIEVEMENT!

⚽ Named in **ESPN's 21 Under 21 list of footballers** representing the next generation of talent

WINS &

⚽ Second in **NXGN Football's 2022 Women's Next Generation** shortlist

⚽ Nominated for **The Best FIFA Women's Player** and **The European Golden Girl Award** in 2023

NOMS

⚽ Second **most-googled** person in Australia in 2023

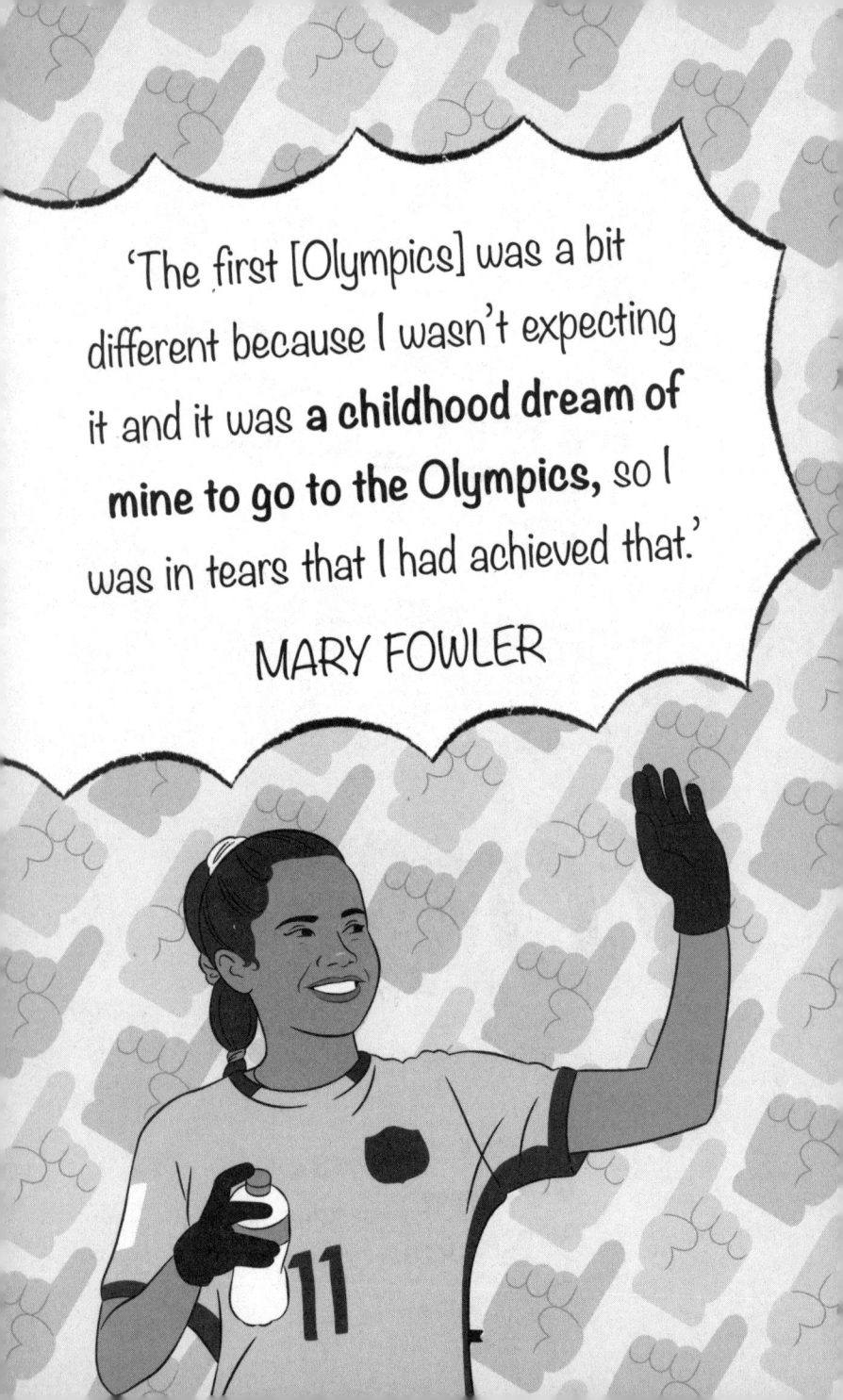

'The first [Olympics] was a bit different because I wasn't expecting it and it was **a childhood dream of mine to go to the Olympics**, so I was in tears that I had achieved that.'

MARY FOWLER

CHAPTER NINE

FOWLER FEVER

There was a **MASSIVE** **build-up** to the **2023 FIFA Women's World Cup.** For the first time ever, it was going to be held in **Australia** and **New Zealand.**

Mary was being called **Australia's 'rising star'**, and even the **Matildas captain, Sam Kerr,** was calling Mary **THE NEXT BIG THING.**

The pressure was on!

LEGENDARY GAME

⚽ WHAT?
World Cup GOOOOAL

⚽ WHO?
Matildas vs Canada

⚽ WHERE?
AAMI Park, Melbourne, Australia

Why was it LEGENDARY?

The Matildas pulled off a remarkable **4-0 victory** over **Olympic champions Canada!**

Mary smashed the ball into the top of the net from close range, but the goal was disallowed after VAR review. But **she tried again and scored her first World Cup goal in the second half.**

UP THE TILLIES!!!

LEGENDARY GAME

⚽ WHAT?
Mary's Magic Moment

⚽ WHO?
Matildas vs Denmark

⚽ WHERE?
Accor Stadium, Sydney, Australia

Why was it LEGENDARY?

The **Matildas won 2-0 against Denmark.** Mary was playing down the other end in the Denmark half when the ball came to her. **She kicked a left-footed through ball** to teammate **Caitlin Foord,** who immediately **scored a goal.**

A **CENTIMETRE-PERFECT pass,** and on to the quarterfinals!

LEGENDARY GAME

⚽ WHAT?
Shoutout Showdown

⚽ WHO?
Matildas vs France

⚽ WHERE?
Lang Park, Brisbane, Australia

⚽ WHY WAS IT LEGENDARY?
In the quarterfinals against France, Mary had to do her first penalty shootout in the tournament...

First, she stared down France's goalkeeper **Solène Durand,**

then **she bounced the ball twice** like a basketballer,

then **she took two steps back** and **breathed in deep,**

then **she breathed out, took two light steps forward...**

And **SMASHED** the ball low and hard into the **left corner of the net.**

The French goalkeeper never had a chance!

It was a **PERFECT PENALTY.**

The Matildas lost to England in the semi-finals and placed fourth in the tournament.

KIRA KIRA
The Home of
MARY BOIO

In **Kira Kira,** her mother **Nido's** village, watch parties were held during **the World Cup** and everyone gathered together **to enjoy the games on a little television.**

There was a **big banner** hanging in the street that said…

VILLAGE
Koita Maiyago
FOWLER

'Koita Maiyago' means 'Girl from our tribe'

⚽ People noticed that Mary **wasn't wearing her gloves** as much.

⚽ She said it's **too hot to wear gloves in warmer countries,** so she wears a **hair tie** around her hand and fiddles with that instead.

I'm not wearing my gloves anymore either. They were DELICIOUS!

'Being selected was a **massive honour.** The last **World Cup,** I didn't get any minutes, but it was still an amazing experience. Just being there with the girls **gave me so much motivation** to want to be there for the next one and **play a bigger role.'**

MARY FOWLER

CHAPTER TEN

THE LEGENDARY MARY FOWLER

Mary has come so far on the field in such a short time, and she just **keeps getting BETTER.**

The Matildas qualified for the **Paris 2024 Olympics.** This would be Mary's **fifth major tournament!**

Despite their best efforts, they didn't make it to the quarterfinals, but the **team has their eyes on the next Olympic Games.**

Bring on L.A. 2028!

When she's not playing, Mary wants to spend more time in **Papua New Guinea.** She has only visited her mum's homeland once, but she has a **dream** to set up a **football academy** or a **school** there one day.

'It's just special to see **how much they support me** and how much they **believe in me** and **look up to me**…If being able to do some **football stuff brings joy** to some people there, then that would be amazing, because there's just **so many good people** out there. I would love to be able to **connect with my mum's roots** a lot more and s**pend time with her family** over there as well.'

MARY FOWLER

Mary has been a part of some **amazing teams,** and she can now add to the list:

TEAM BARBIE

In **2024,** the company that makes Barbie **created a doll that looks like Mary** as part of a campaign to celebrate how sports builds **self-confidence, ambition** and **empowerment.**

'I wanted to have my **Barbie doll** replicate when I feel my **most confident self,** and that for me is when I'm on the pitch **playing football.** To finally hold my doll and see her wear my **bubble braid, my gloves,** and even my **boots,** made my Barbie doll **unique** and **connected** to me.'

MARY FOWLER

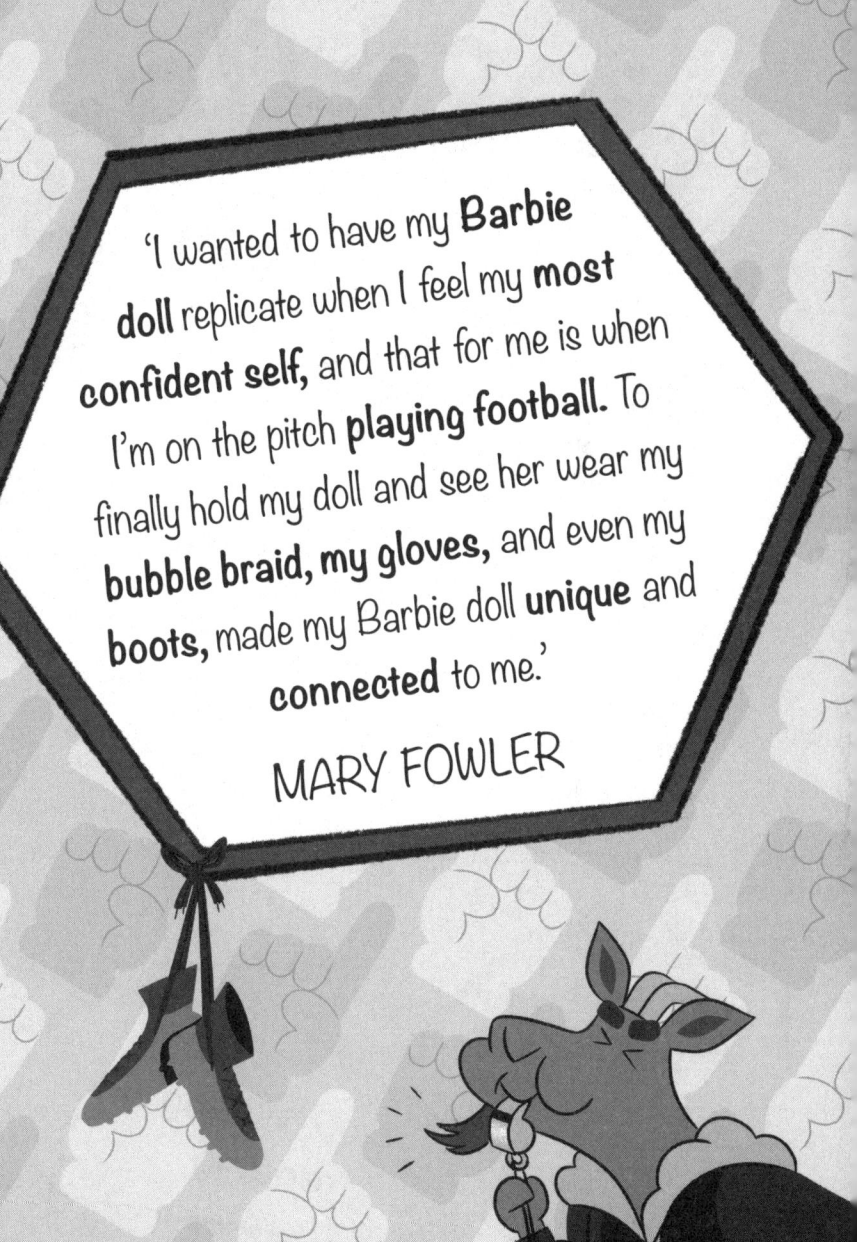

Things Mary

- Cappuccinos and practising latte art
- Scrambled eggs and baked beans on toast for breakfast
- Drawing
- Writing and reading

Fowler loves

⚽ Jazz music

⚽ Mary might **open up a café** once she's done with soccer. She could call it **Tillies Tea-Time** or **Double-shot Mary!**

THE LEGENDARY MARY FOWLER

Can play with both feet

Fifteen goals for the Matildas

The fifth-youngest player for the Matildas

Over 50 appearances for Australia

Second most-googled Australian in 2023, behind teammate and captain Sam Kerr

There is no doubt: **Mary Fowler** is a true

SPORTING LEGEND!

Gary's Knowledge Knockout

1. What country did the Fowler family move to when Mary was ten years old?

2. What was Mary's favourite subject at school?

3. What is the name of the village in Papua New Guinea where Mary's mum was born?

4. What do they call 'soccer' in England?

5. Against which team did Mary score her first Olympic goal?

6. Mary likes writing and drawing. True or False?

7. Why was Mary's first professional game for Adelaide United soccer team extra special?

8. Why does Mary sometimes wear gloves during a match?

9. Which country wanted Mary to play for its soccer team before Mary decided to join the Matildas?

10. What happens if a player is shown a red card by the referee?

ANSWERS:
1. The Netherlands **2.** Maths **3.** Kira Kira **4.** Football **5.** Great Britain **6.** True **7.** It was also her sister, Ciara's, first professional game **8.** She gets fidgety **9.** Ireland **10.** The player is sent off the field for the rest of the game for breaking the rules

GARY'S TOP TERMS

Kickoff: When a player kicks the ball to a teammate from the centre circle. This happens at the start of a match, at the start of halftime and after a goal.

Own goal: When a player accidentally kicks the ball into their own goal net, which scores a point for the other team.

Volley: When a player kicks the ball while it's mid-air.

Caught sleeping: When you're not concentrating on your job and make a silly mistake that could have been easily avoided.

Clean sheet: When a team manages to not give away a single goal for the whole match.

Hoofing the ball: When you kick the ball as hard as possible in the general direction of the opposition's goal.

Sitter: When a player misses a huge chance to score, often when the ball has been put on a plate for them.

Punt: A drop kick of the ball, usually done by the goalie.

Bottling it: When a team has thrown away a game from a position of advantage.

Golden goal: A method of deciding a game that has gone into extra time – the team which scores first wins!

Off the woodwork: When a ball hits the post or crossbar. The term is a throwback to a time when goalposts were made out of wood.

More FACTS, more STATS, more LEGENDS!

F1 LEGENDS
DANIEL RICCIARDO
STATS! FACTS! STORIES!
KIT CROSS & LEIGH HEDSTROM

FOOTBALL LEGENDS
SAM KERR
STATS! FACTS! STORIES!
HEDSTROM

BASKETBALL LEGENDS
BEN SIMMONS
& LEIGH HEDSTROM

OUT NOW

legendsofsportbooks.com.au